Earthworms

This edition first published in 2005 by
Sea-to-Sea Publications
1980 Lookout Drive
North Mankato
Minnesota 56003

ISBN   1-932889-20-5

Printed in China

Library of Congress Control Number:
2004103612

2 4 6 8 9 7 5 3

Published by arrangement with the
Watts Publishing Group Ltd, London

Design: Ben White
Consultant: C. H. Keeling

KEEPING MINIBEASTS

Earthworms

TEXT: CHRIS HENWOOD

PHOTOGRAPHS: BARRIE WATTS

CONTENTS

SEA-TO-SEA

Mankato Collingwood London

Introduction

Have you ever thought about keeping an earthworm as a pet?

Worms are very easy creatures to find. You can dig them up in almost any piece of soil that is cool and moist.

Worms are very easy to find after rain in the spring and fall. But they are often harder to find in very hot or cold weather.

If the weather is dry when you are looking for your worms, try watering the soil and leaving it for a few hours. This will encourage the worms to come to the surface as they think it has rained.

In cold weather you may be able to get the same thing to happen if you cover a piece of soil with a large stone.

Worms come in many
different shapes and
sizes. Don't worry as
they will all live well
together. It may be
nice to get worms
from different places.

Before you start collecting worms you should have a place in which to keep them. You can use a tall jar or even a sandwich box with holes punched into the lid.

You can't see worms very well in these plastic boxes. Why not make a very special place for them to stay in? It's called a terrarium.

Making a terrarium

Ask an adult to help. You will need two sheets of plastic or glass, three pieces of wood, two nails and some strong tape.

Nail the long pieces of wood to the shorter piece as shown. Tape the glass or plastic to the wood to make a tall, narrow box.

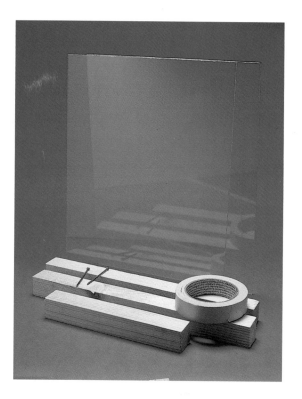

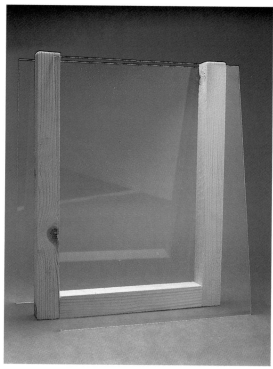

Once you have done this fill the box with soil. Earthworms feed on the decaying plants found on or near the soil surface.

Always keep your terrarium cool and moist. Be careful not to make it too wet or your worms may drown.

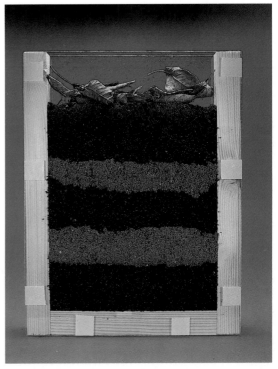

Place your worms on top of the soil. They will soon begin to burrow down into it, moving away from the light. They will come back when it's dark to collect food.

In addition to the food already in the soil, every six weeks or so, add a small amount of oatmeal and a few decaying leaves as food.

Parts of a worm

Before you put your worm into its new home, look at it closely. Notice the rings or segments of the body. What does the worm feel like? You will see how wet it is. A worm needs to keep its body moist so that it can move through the soil.

Can you see that each segment is covered in tiny little hairs?

These hairs help the worm move along both through the soil and on the ground.

Worms burrowing

If you want to see how much your worms move about and eat, place a layer of sand between two areas of soil in your terrarium. You will then see how much they have moved by the mixing of the soil. You must cover the glass with either dark paper or cloth.

Earthworms are able to push objects that are ten times their own weight.

A worm moves by stretching its body in the direction it wants to go. It contracts then stretches out again.

As it moves like this it will appear to get fatter and thinner with each movement. Earthworms will move up and down in the soil when it is cold, covering distances between one and two yards.

When you place your worm on the surface of the soil it will soon begin to burrow down into it. As it does so, the worm sucks earth in and digests the food items it needs.

The worm leaves the rest of the earth behind.
The earth that is left behind is known as a cast.
  It is these casts that you can sometimes
see on grass. They can tell you that worms
are working away under your feet.

Baby worms

Part of an adult worm's body is called a "saddle." In this picture it is pinker and fatter than the rest of the worm. Each worm is both male and female but two worms must join up to make sure sperm and eggs are mixed. The "saddle" makes a sticky mixture when the two worms join. Then the "saddle" becomes a

kind of capsule and is pushed along and away from the worm. It forms a cocoon, often left just under the soil. Young worms hatch out from it after a few weeks.

When you go away you don't have to worry about finding someone to look after your pets.

You can just let your worms go back into the garden or area of soil from which you first got them. Naturally, you will not be able to do this if the soil is very dry or frosty.

All you have to do is dig a little hole and put your worms into it, then cover over gently with loose soil. This will keep birds from finding them.

Unusual facts

There are over 1,800 different species of earthworms all over the world.

The largest earthworm ever found was in South Africa and measured 22 feet (6.7 m) from nose to tail tip.

They are part of a large group of animals called invertebrates – which means they do not have backbones. They are also called annelids, which refers to the many rings or segments that make up the body.

Earthworms are extremely valuable creatures as they keep the soil healthy, well-aired and drained through their constant burrowing. They eat the soil and form casts which then make very good topsoil.

Index